A Little Book for

GRANDMOTHER

Andrews McMeel
Publishing, LLC

Kansas City

A Little Book for Grandmother

For information, write Andrews McMeel Publishing, LLC, an Andrews McMeel Universal company, 4520 Main Street, Kansas City, Missouri 64111.

07 08 09 10 11 TEP 10 9 8 7 6 5 4 3 2 1

ISBN-13: 978-0-7407-6407-3
ISBN-10: 0-7407-6407-1

Library of Congress Control Number: 2006933027

Compiled by Patrick Regan

www.andrewsmcmeel.com

ATTENTION: SCHOOLS AND BUSINESSES

Andrews McMeel books are available at quantity discounts with bulk purchase for educational, business, or sales promotional use. For information, please write to: Special Sales Department, Andrews McMeel Publishing, LLC, 4520 Main Street, Kansas City, Missouri 64111.

Introduction

Grandchildren are the dots that connect the lines from generation to generation.

—Lois Wyse

Grandmothers are not what they used to be. The traditional image of a plump, silver-haired woman coming out of the kitchen, wiping flour-covered hands on her apron, is as worn and faded as farmhouse curtains. Today's grandmother is just as likely to go on a five-mile bike ride with her grandkids as to whip up a batch of cookies each time they visit.

But the essence of being a grandma hasn't changed and surely never will. To grandchildren, a grandmother represents that perfect balance of wisdom and warmth. Grandmothers seem to have seen all and know all and yet have a knack for making their grandchildren feel like they themselves are the most remarkable people they've ever known.

No matter what hardships a grandmother has faced in her life, she will always reserve the softest spot in her heart for her grandchildren. For the young ones, no place is as comforting as her lap, and as grow older, they find that grandmother seems to have a ready and wise answer to every question.

If the happiest day of a woman's life is the day she becomes a mother, the second-happiest day must surely be when she first becomes a grandmother. The pride and love, warmth and affection she first felt so long ago comes flowing back in waves—and it never really stops flowing. It washes over her grandchildren forever. That's something about grandmothers that will never change. 🖤

If I had known
how wonderful it
would be to have
grandchildren,
I'd have had
them first.

Lois Wyse

A grandma's name
is little less in love
than is the doting
title of a mother.

William Shakespeare

Becoming a grandmother is wonderful. One moment you're just a mother. The next you are all-wise and prehistoric.

Pam Brown

I loved their home.
Everything smelled
older, worn but safe;
the food aroma had
baked itself into
the furniture.

Susan Strasberg

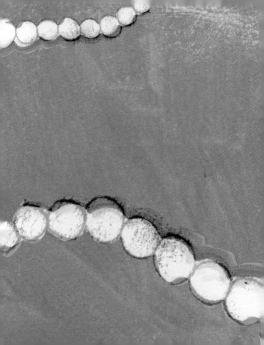

If God had
intended us to
follow recipes, he
wouldn't have given
us grandmothers.

Linda Henley

Her grandmother,
as she gets older,
is not fading but
rather becoming
more concentrated.

Paulette Bates Alden

Everyone needs
to have access both
to grandparents and
grandchildren in
order to be a full
human being.

Margaret Mead

We should all have one person who knows how to bless us despite the evidence. Grandmother was that person to me.

Phyllis Theroux

It's one of nature's ways that we often feel closer to distant generations than to the generation immediately preceding us.

Igor Stravinsky

It is as grandmothers
that our mothers
come into the
fullness of
their grace.

Christopher Morley

You do not
really understand
something unless
you can explain it to
your grandmother.

Proverb

Most grandmas have a touch of the scallywag.

Helen Thomson

It's amazing how grandparents seem so young once you become one.

Anonymous

Few things are more delightful than grandchildren fighting over your lap.

Doug Larson

Grandmother-grandchild relationships are simple. Grandmas are short on criticism and long on love.

Anonymous

Grandma always made you feel like she had been waiting to see just you all day, and now the day was complete.

Marcy DeMaree

A mother becomes a true grandmother the day she stops noticing the terrible things her children do because she is so enchanted with the wonderful things her grandchildren do.

Lois Wyse

Uncles and aunts and cousins are all very well, and fathers and mothers are not to be despised, but a grandmother, at holiday time, is worth them all.

Fanny Fern

Our grandchildren accept us for ourselves, without rebuke or effort to change us, as no one in our entire lives has ever done, not our parents, siblings, spouses, friends—and hardly ever our own grown children.

Ruth Goode

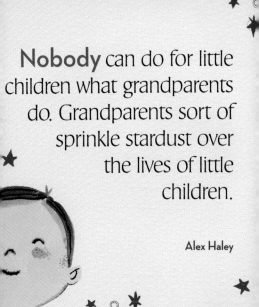

Nobody can do for little children what grandparents do. Grandparents sort of sprinkle stardust over the lives of little children.

Alex Haley

If becoming a grandmother was only a matter of choice, I should advise every one of you straight away to become one. There is no fun for old people like it!

Hannah Whithall Smith

When grandparents
enter the door,
discipline flies
out the window.

Ogden Nash

Have children while
your parents are still
young enough to take
care of them.

Rita Rudner

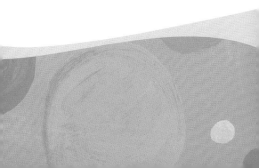

A grandmother
pretends she
doesn't know
who you are
on Halloween.

Erma Bombeck

Grandparents are similar to a piece of string—handy to have around and easily wrapped around the fingers of their grandchildren.

Anonymous

Just about the time a woman thinks her work is done, she becomes a grandmother.

Edward H. Dreschnack

My grandmother is over eighty and still doesn't need glasses. Drinks right out of the bottle.

Henny Youngman

No cowboy was ever faster on the draw than a grandparent pulling a baby picture out of a wallet.

Anonymous

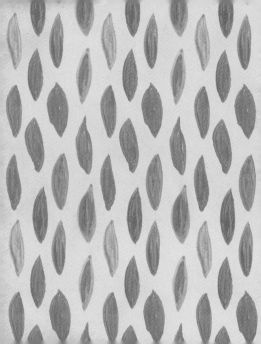

Grandchildren
are God's way of
compensating us
for growing old.

Mary H. Waldrip

The simplest toy, one which even the youngest child can operate, is called a grandparent.

Sam Levenson

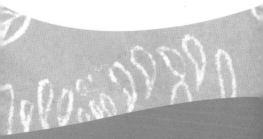

If your baby is "beautiful and perfect, never cries or fusses, sleeps on schedule and burps on demand, an angel all the time," you're the grandma.

Teresa Bloomingdale

What is it about grandparents that is so lovely? I'd like to say that grandparents are God's gifts to children. And if they can but see, hear, and feel what these people have to give, they can mature at a fast rate.

Bill Cosby

The closest friends
I have made all
through life have
been people who
also grew up
close to a loved
and living
grandmother
or grandfather.

Margaret Mead

If you want to civilize a man, begin with his grandmother.

Victor Hugo

A **house** needs a grandma in it.

Louisa May Alcott

What children need most are the essentials that grandparents provide in abundance. They give unconditional love, kindness, patience, humor, comfort, lessons in life. And, most importantly, cookies.

Rudolph Giuliani

Being pretty on the inside means you don't hit your brother and you eat all your peas—that's what my grandma taught me.

Lord Chesterfield

A grandmother is a
little bit parent, a
little bit teacher,
and a little bit
best friend.

Anonymous

A grandmother is a babysitter who watches the kids instead of the television.

Anonymous

If nothing is going well, call your grandmother.

Italian proverb

Elephants and grandchildren never forget.

Andy Rooney